The Cuban Missile Crisis

President Kennedy's Address to the Nation

October 22, 1962

MILESTONE DOCUMENTS IN THE NATIONAL ARCHIVES

National Archives and Records Administration

Washington, DC

Published for the
National Archives and Records Administration
By the National Archives Trust Fund Board
1988

Library of Congress Cataloging-in-Publication Data

Kennedy, John F. (John Fitzgerald), 1917-1963.
    The Cuban missile crisis.

    (Milestone documents in the National Archives)
    Bibliography: p.
    1. Cuban Missile Crisis, Oct. 1962. I. United
States. National Archives and Records Administration.
II. Title. III. Series.
E838.5.K45   1988   973.922   88-600062
ISBN 0-911333-59-2

An Introduction

When President John F. Kennedy came before the television cameras on that fateful Monday evening of October 22, 1962, he presented a speech that would place the United States and the Soviet Union on the brink of thermonuclear disaster. Only one week before, he had received proof that the Soviets had placed medium-range nuclear weapons in Cuba, just 90 miles from U.S. soil, and were making them operational.

On October 20, U.S. armed forces worldwide had been placed on alert. Secretary of Defense Robert S. McNamara had ordered four tactical air squadrons to be ready for an air strike over Cuban missile sites, airfields, ports, and gun emplacements. More than 100,000 troops were being deployed into Florida in preparation for a possible land invasion of Cuba following an air strike. The U.S. naval base at Guantanamo Bay, Cuba, where 5,000 Marines were already stationed, had been strengthened. The Navy also sent 180 vessels into the Caribbean for a previously planned amphibious exercise spearheaded by 40,000 Marines. The Strategic Air Command had been deployed to civilian landing fields throughout the country in order to reduce its vulnerability to possible retaliatory strikes by the Soviets. In addition, the B-52 bomber force had been ordered into the air fully loaded with atomic weapons; as one plane landed and refueled, another immediately took its place in the sky.

Each of the 42 Soviet medium-range ballistic missiles already in Cuba was capable of striking the United States with a nuclear warhead 20 to 30 times more destructive than that which had destroyed Hiroshima. The Soviets had surveyed and selected launch sites, brought in protective antiaircraft missiles, improved roads, and evicted local inhabitants. Even as President Kennedy delivered his address, several of the launch pads were nearing completion. The medium-range missiles would be operational in less than a week, additional intermediate-range ballistic missiles by early December. These missiles would increase the Soviet Union's overall nuclear strike capacity by 50 percent, resulting in a dramatic shift in the nuclear balance.

The strain in U.S.–Soviet relations had been escalating dangerously for some time. The construction of the Berlin Wall in August 1961 and the series of atmospheric nuclear tests by both powers had increased tensions and raised the specter of eventual confrontation. When Fidel Castro, after successfully leading a revolution in Cuba against the Batista government in 1958–59, cultivated relations with the Soviet Union, the United States was suddenly confronted with the presence of a Marxist nation off its shores.

On January 3, 1961, the United States broke off diplomatic relations with Cuba. Three months later, about 1,500 Cuban exiles who had been trained and equipped by the Central Intelligence Agency invaded Cuba at the Bay of Pigs. They were quickly overcome by Castro's forces and compelled to surrender. Later, on January 3, 1962, the White House released the text of a statement that had been made on December 6, 1961, in which Cuba had been described as a "bridgehead of Sino-Soviet imperialism and a base for communist agitation and subversion within the inner defense of the Western Hemisphere."

By the summer of 1962, significant movements of Soviet personnel and equipment into Cuba had aroused the suspicions of our intelligence community. After a series of meetings at the White House, U.S. Navy ships and planes began to photograph every Soviet vessel bound for Cuba. U-2 reconnaissance flights covered the entire island twice monthly. A special daily intelligence report began on August 27.

Photographs taken on August 29 and reported to the President on August 31 provided the first hard evidence that antiaircraft surface-to-air missiles (SAMs), missile-equipped torpedo boats for coastal defense, and substantial numbers of Soviet military personnel had arrived in Cuba. Neither these photos, however, nor those taken on September 5 produced evidence of offensive ballistic missiles. At the time, only CIA Chief John McCone speculated that the SAM sites might be intended to protect offensive missile installations. Other Presidential advisers

By fall, the Soviets had transported to Cuba forty-two medium-range ballistic missiles (MRBMs) — each one capable of striking the U.S. with a nuclear warhead 20 to 30 times more destructive than the one employed at Hiroshima. Intermediate-range ballistic missiles (IRBMs), with a longer-range of 2,200 miles, would be capable of reaching virtually any part of the continental United States. Khrushchev, in his memoirs, noted that by October 22, missile installations capable of destroying New York, Chicago, Washington, and other major American cities had already become operative. (167803 USAF, DOD Still Media Depository)

Photos of a ballistic-missile launch site at San Cristobal, Cuba, provided the first indisputable evidence of Soviet offensive-missile deployment, October 14, 1962. From that point forward, President Kennedy took a position from which he never deviated: the missiles would have to be removed. (Dept. of Defense PX66-20:7, JFK Library)

discounted this possibility because the Soviets had never deployed missiles outside of Soviet territory, not even in Eastern Europe where they could be easily guarded and supplied. Why would the U.S.S.R. risk U.S. intervention in Cuba and expose Castro's regime to danger?

The Soviets, particularly after the Bay of Pigs, believed that another land invasion of Cuba was inevitable, and sooner or later, U.S. attention would return to this island. In choosing this time to build their missile site in Cuba, the Soviets hoped that the hurricane season would interfere with U-2 flights and that the upcoming congressional elections might impede swift, courageous action by the President. Khrushchev later claimed that his main aim was to free Cuba from a standing threat of invasion from the United States and that in this he succeeded.

While American U-2 surveillance planes were grounded or rendered ineffective due to bad weather (until September 26), President Kennedy delivered two explicit warnings to Khrushchev regarding the build-up of ostensibly defensive Soviet arms in Cuba. On September 4 he stated that although he had no evidence of "significant offensive capacity either in Cuban hands or under Soviet direction," should it prove otherwise, "the gravest issues would arise." Two weeks later, on September 13, Kennedy reaffirmed that

> If at any time the Communist build-up in Cuba were to endanger or interfere with our security in any way . . . or if Cuba should ever . . . become an offensive military base of significant capacity for the Soviet Union, then this country will do whatever must be done to protect its own security and that of its allies.

Reconnaissance flights resumed on September 26 and 29 and October 5 and 7. After another week of delay caused by bad weather, U-2 planes flew through a cloudless sky over Cuba early Sunday morning, October 14. By Monday afternoon, the aerial photographs had been analyzed and re-analyzed. There could no longer be any doubt about Soviet intentions in Cuba. The rude beginnings of a Soviet medium-range ballistic missile base had been discovered near San Cristobal. When confronted with the evidence, the President's mind was immediately set — the missiles would have to be removed.

That Tuesday morning, October 16, the President called together his most trusted advisers to serve as an Executive Committee of the National Security Council. ExComm, as this group became known, was charged with presenting the President with possible responses to the missile build-up and their projected consequences. No one in the ExComm believed at the outset that they could come up with a permanent solution. They might prolong the stand-off, perhaps indefinitely, or they might run the risk of forcing one side or the other to resort to the use of nuclear weapons. It was the first direct nuclear confrontation in history, and the President needed the best, most dispassionate advice possible. Each man was being asked to make a recommendation that, if wrong and accepted, could mean the end of the human race. The responsibility for the ultimate decision, however, lay with the President.

The CIA estimated that the missiles would be operational within two weeks. In the ExComm meetings, many "solutions" were presented, dissected, reassembled, and broken down again to bare essentials. Several were discussed and laid aside. The alternatives discussed most seriously included doing nothing, working through the United Nations and the Organization of American States, offering to remove our missiles in Turkey in exchange for the removal of those in Cuba, sending secret envoys to Castro, blockading Cuba, striking Cuba by air (with or without warning), and launching a land invasion. Eventually, the committee focused more and more on a naval blockade.

On one hand, a blockade seemed irrelevant to the whole problem. It would not eliminate the missiles, and it could antagonize our allies who were sensitive to the freedom of the seas. If the OAS declared the blockade illegal, as a violation of the U.N. Charter and international law, the Soviets might gain a "mandate" to disregard it. Moreover, U.S. forces might be manipulated into firing the first shot of what could develop into war. In the meantime, the missiles would become operational. At best, the naval blockade seemed to offer a prolonged and agonizing approach, uncertain in effect and indefinite in duration. All of these factors would make it more difficult to stage a later air strike and land invasion.

Yet, the superiority of the U.S. Navy over the Soviet Navy on the high seas was indisputable. If Khrushchev turned his ships back, our allies would be encouraged, and Castro might begin to feel abandoned.

If nothing was done, the world would soon know that the Kennedy administration had allowed the Soviets to erect offensive weapons in the United States' own backyard capable of killing 50 million Americans in a matter of minutes. With congressional elections scheduled for the following week, there was concern that a "hawkish" Republican majority might win control of the House of Representatives. The ability of the administration to respond effectively to crises would thereafter be paralyzed.

On Thursday, October 18, President Kennedy met for two hours with Soviet Foreign Minister Andrei A. Gromyko. Gromyko focused on Berlin, skirting the subject of Cuba. When the foreign minister finally mentioned Cuba, he stressed that nation's fears of an American invasion and spoke against acts of U.S. interference. These actions, Gromyko charged, were unprovoked acts of aggression that threatened to lead us into war. Soviet weapons in Cuba were "by no means offensive," he said. "If it were otherwise, the Soviet Government would

The crisis begins. President John F. Kennedy delivers his "Report to the American People on the Soviet Arms Buildup in Cuba," on national television, October 22, 1962. The U.S. Information Agency prepared special hookups with radio stations that carried the President's speech, in Spanish, to Cuba and throughout Latin America. (KN24679, JFK Library)

have never become involved in rendering such assistance." In response, the President asked for and read to Gromyko his September 4 statement that sharply warned against offensive missiles in Cuba.

Preparations began that evening for a proclamation of a blockade and for numerous complementary actions. By Friday morning, however, the blockade plan had not yet won unanimous support. The Joint Chiefs of Staff continued to advocate an air strike and land invasion, and other top advisers expressed doubts about the effectiveness of a blockade. Time was growing short, and the President was obliged to leave for a midwestern campaign tour. He could not risk the questions and suspicions that would arise from a sudden change in his itinerary. As he headed out, he was discouraged and becoming impatient. He wanted to act on Sunday. Nevertheless, all options once again underwent close scrutiny.

While the President was away, the ExComm met at 11 a.m. on October 19. Back and forth went the challenges. Secretary McNamara spoke firmly in favor of the blockade and against an air attack. Attorney General Robert F. Kennedy, speaking with quiet intensity, raised the argument that a Sunday morning surprise attack on a very small country would betray our nation's heritage and ideals. The

President of the United States could not with impunity order such an operation. Kennedy later recalled that the ExComm spent more time discussing this issue than any other single matter. His remarks reminded those at the meeting that more was at stake than the mere physical survival of this nation. In retrospect, most participants agreed that Robert Kennedy's speech marked the turning point in the ExComm discussions.

When the group met Friday afternoon, it drew up concrete arguments against an air strike. Late that night and into Saturday morning, Theodore Sorensen, Special Counsel to the President and his principal speechwriter, wrote out a workable draft speech. At 9 a.m. on Saturday, October 20, the draft was quickly "reviewed, amended, and generally approved." Shortly after 10 a.m., Robert Kennedy telephoned the President and asked him to return from Chicago.

When the President returned to the White House at about 1:30 p.m., Sorensen familiarized him with the speech. At 2:30 the ExComm met for the first time officially as the National Security Council. At the meeting, proponents of both the air strike and blockade strategies presented their best arguments to the President. "Essentially, Mr. President," one adviser said, "this is a choice between limited action and unlimited action; and most of us think that it's better to start with limited action." Kennedy nodded in full agreement.

The President wanted the speech to clarify that the confrontation was between the nuclear powers and not between the United States and Castro. Furthermore, he wished to emphasize that an air strike and invasion were not being ruled out for the future. Yet, the President did not want to corner the Russians into a choice between "humiliating retreat or nuclear war." The blockade left Khrushchev with choices that an air strike probably would not have permitted

Post-October 23 detail of San Cristobal site. On October 25, low-flying reconnaissance flights reported that construction of the launch sites in Cuba continued at a frenetic pace. On October 27, one U.S. pilot was shot down and killed while others reported that the Russians were working day and night to complete work on missile sites and the IL-28s bombers. (Dept. of Defense PX66-20:20, JFK Library)

— at least our chosen course of action would not kill a single Soviet or Cuban citizen. President Kennedy reaffirmed the decision to stop only surface ships and not deter imports of petroleum, oil, and lubricants. Such an action would have been regarded as an overt attempt to collapse the Castro regime and distract attention from the nuclear warheads. The President chose the term "quarantine" rather than "blockade" as more appropriate to an act of peaceful self-preservation.

During the meeting, the President stated, "The worst course of all would be for us to do nothing." Sorensen later recalled making a mental note to add that sentence to the speech. "There isn't any good solution. . . . But this one [the blockade] seems the least objectionable," Kennedy decided. Those who had advocated the air strike/invasion were essentially won over by the President's plan of action. Bitter disagreement, however, broke out over the diplomatic moves to accompany it. Many proposals, even that of making outright concessions to the Russians, were discussed. It became clear to the President that instead of being on the diplomatic defensive, we should be indicting the Soviet Union for its duplicity and for threatening world peace. That thought set the tenor for his speech.

When all seemed settled, the President declared that he wanted to speak on the following evening. The State Department, however, stressed the importance of briefing Latin American leaders, our ambassadors, and allies, and the difficulty of reaching them all on a Sunday. Kennedy agreed to delay his speech until Monday, but he kept Sunday open in case secrecy crumbled and news of his plan leaked out. Regardless of the response from our allies, he intended to present the "quarantine" to the world as a *fait accompli* at 7 p.m. Monday evening.

The speech and quarantine proclamation, along with draft letters to heads of state, the OAS, the Mayor of West Berlin, and Khrushchev, were circulated and reworked. The United States Information Agency prepared a special hookup with private radio stations to carry the President's speech in Spanish to Cuba and all of Latin America. Former Secretary of State Dean Acheson had earlier in the week suggested sending a special high-level emissary to brief DeGaulle and NATO, and he himself was given that assignment. Military preparations for all levels of action continued.

On Sunday morning, October 21, Sorensen incorporated suggested changes into a fourth draft of the speech. At that time, Tactical Air Command Chief, Gen. Walter C. Sweeney, Jr., informed the President that there was no way of making certain that all the missiles could be removed by "surgical" air attack. A strike, therefore, left open the possibility of nuclear retaliation. Khrushchev, in his memoirs, recorded that by speech-time missile installations capable of destroying New York, Chicago, Washington, and other industrial cities had already become operational. A massive air strike by the United States would appear excessive to our European allies, who had long lived under the shadow of nuclear weapons, and it would cause a huge and unconscionable loss of life.

The President made dozens of alterations both great and small to Sorensen's latest draft. He deleted a call for a summit meeting, preferring to state generally that the United States was prepared to present its case in any appropriate forum at any time. Kennedy did not want to be obligated to any particular course of diplomatic action. The President wished to concentrate on the seriousness of the missiles' presence and the absolute necessity for their removal.

> We no longer live in a world where only the actual firing of weapons represents a sufficient challenge to a nation's security to constitute maximum peril. Nuclear weapons are so destructive, and ballistic missiles are so swift, that any substantially increased possibility of their use or any sudden change in their deployment may well be regarded as a definite threat to peace.

Soviet assurances from September and October were recounted in the speech, and after each one the President inserted the words, "That statement was false."

The speech also contained a direct appeal to the Cuban people. President Kennedy called for the day when Cubans

> will truly be free — free from foreign domination, free to choose their own leaders, free to select their own system, free to own their own land, free to speak and write and worship without fear or degradation.

Although including this statement, the President struck out any remarks that were hostile and directed toward Castro, and the Cuban leader's removal from power was not even alluded to. Focus remained on the removal of the Soviet missiles. There was no mistaking the tone of his ultimate pronouncement:

> It shall be the policy of this nation to regard any nuclear missile launched from Cuba against any nation in the Western Hemisphere as an attack by the Soviet Union on the United States, requiring a full retaliatory response upon the Soviet Union.

The text of the speech continued to be changed throughout most of Monday, October 22, each one rushed to USIA translators and to the State Department for transmission to our embassies. At noon the White House announced that at 7 p.m. the President would deliver a speech of the "highest national urgency."

That same morning Kennedy met with the ExComm, and in the afternoon with the full NSC. The President met briefly with his Cabinet about 4 p.m. to explain what he was doing and promptly adjourned the meeting.

"Ex Comm" meeting, October 29, 1962. The day before, Khrushchev had agreed to remove Soviet missiles from Cuba. Seated clockwise from the President: Robert McNamara, Roswell Gilpatric, Gen. Maxwell Taylor, Paul Nitze, Don Wilson, Theodore Sorenson, McGeorge Bundy (hidden), Douglas Dillon, Vice-President Johnson (hidden), Robert Kennedy, Llewellyn Thompson, William C. Foster, John McCone (hidden), George Ball, and Dean Rusk. (ST-A26-1-62, JFK Library)

At 5 p.m. Kennedy met with congressional leaders who had been called back from campaign tours and vacation spots scattered across the country. Senator Richard Russell of Georgia argued vociferously for a more drastic response than the President planned to deliver. But Kennedy told the Congressmen that he was acting by Executive Order, Presidential proclamation, and inherent powers and was not bound to wait for a resolution of Congress. He was not requesting a formal declaration of war: policy was already fixed. The meeting dragged on past 6 p.m. Just before airtime, Kennedy reviewed the text one final time, and then he spoke to an anxious world.

"Our unswerving objective," the President stated, "was to end the nuclear threat to Americans." He laid before the world his initial plan of action: a weapons quarantine; intensified surveillance of Cuba; an immediate convening of the OAS to consider the threat to hemispheric security; an emergency meeting of the United Nations Security Council to consider the threat to world peace; and an appeal to Khrushchev "to abandon this course of world domination, and to join in an historic effort to end the perilous arms race and to transform the history of man." He concluded:

> My fellow citizens: let no one doubt that this is a difficult and dangerous effort. . . . No one can foresee precisely what course it will take or what costs or casualties will be incurred. . . . But the greatest danger of all would be to do nothing. . . . Our goal is not the victory of might, but the vindication of right — not peace at the expense of freedom, but both peace *and* freedom, here in this hemisphere, and, we hope, around the world. God willing, that goal will be achieved.

* * * * *

THE CUBAN MISSILE CRISIS: THE DAYS FOLLOWING KENNEDY'S ADDRESS

With the President's address to the nation, the Cuban missile crisis entered its public phase. During the following week, fear gripped the nation as Americans anxiously waited for each new development. The belief that the United States and the Soviet Union might be drawn into nuclear war became more and more widespread. Both sides worked feverishly to avert such a disaster. Finally, six days after Kennedy's speech, public action and private dialogue brought about a peaceful conclusion to the crisis.

Tuesday, October 23

The OAS and our European allies express unanimous support for the quarantine. Plans continue at the Pentagon for massive air strikes and a land invasion into Cuba.

Khrushchev notifies the United States that the blockade will be ignored and calls our actions toward Cuba "outright banditry or, if you like, the folly of degenerate imperialism." Soviet Ambassador Dobrynin repeats that there are no missiles in Cuba.

Wednesday, October 24

Several Soviet vessels turn back from the quarantine line; those continuing on are mostly tankers. President Kennedy had reduced the 800-mile limit to 500 miles on Tuesday night, and the United States does not stop and search any vessels on the high seas.

UN Ambassador Adlai Stevenson presents photographs of the missiles to the world in a dramatic televised confrontation with Ambassador V. A. Zorin of the

Soviet Union. This evidence of the existence of Soviet missile bases has devastating effects on the Soviets' continued attempts to deny Kennedy's charges.

Thursday, October 25

Low-flying reconnaissance flights begin over Cuba each morning and afternoon. Construction of the missile launch sites continues at a frenetic pace.

Friday, October 26

In a statement strongly petitioning for peace, Khrushchev informs the United States that no Soviet ship bound for Cuba carries any weapons because all armaments are already in Cuba. He adds, "If assurances were given that the President of the United States would not participate in an attack on Cuba and the blockade lifted, then the question of the removal or destruction of the missile sites in Cuba would then be an entirely different question."

John Scali, a reporter for the ABC television network, receives a proposal from an important Soviet Embassy official. It clarifies Khrushchev's position: removal of the missiles under UN supervision and inspection in exchange for lifting the blockade and a pledge not to invade Cuba. The President and members of the ExComm for the first time are hopeful that the crisis might be settled without war.

Saturday, October 27

A new letter is received from the Foreign Office of the Kremlin. It demands our removal of missiles in Turkey in exchange for removal of missiles in Cuba. Clearly, if we invade Cuba, then the Soviet Union would invade Turkey. Action in Turkey would immediately involve all NATO countries, and the President is sobered by the fact that he now finds himself the spokesman for the entire free world.

U-2 pilot Major Rudolf Anderson, Jr., one of the two pilots who uncovered the presence of missiles in Cuba, is shot down over Cuba and killed. New evidence shows that Russians are working day and night to complete work on the missile sites and IL-28 bombers.

The President restrains those who call for the destruction of the missile sites in retaliation. "It isn't the first step that concerns me, but both sides escalating to the fourth and fifth step — and we don't go to the sixth because there is no one around to do so. We must remind ourselves we are embarking on a very hazardous course." Kennedy chooses to respond to the first letter from Khrushchev and accepts his "offer." But U-2 flights continue, and Robert Kennedy meets again with Dobrynin and insists that an answer be returned the next day.

Sunday, October 28

The Soviets agree to withdraw the missiles from Cuba.

Postlude

President Kennedy made no statement attempting to take credit for himself or for his administration for the final result. He gave instructions that no one in his government was to give interviews or make any statements that would claim any sort of victory. He respected Khrushchev for properly determining what was in both his own country's best interest and that of all mankind.

THE FACSIMILES

President Kennedy's reading copy of his REPORT TO THE AMERICAN PEOPLE ON THE SOVIET BUILDUP IN CUBA, OCTOBER 22, 1962. (John F. Kennedy Library)

The following facsimile is of President Kennedy's reading copy of his address concerning the Cuban Missile Crisis. In his actual delivery, he followed this text fairly closely, with most deviations being minor insertions or deletions. In describing the buildup of Soviet arms in Cuba, Kennedy said that "it had been planned for some months" instead of "planned some months ago," as was written in his address. Toward the end of his talk, when the President warned the American people of the difficult times ahead, he transposed the words "will" and "patience" in "our will and our patience will be tested." Kennedy also chose to emphasize certain words or passages. He stressed that the Soviet Union had denied the presence of missiles by inserting "I quote the Soviet government" and "I quote their government" into his recitation of Soviet statements. He also underlined the United States' concern for the Cuban people when he added "and the American people have watched" to "And I have watched with deep sorrow how your nationalist revolution was betrayed." On other occasions he emphasized the words *"attack,"* the Soviet *"government's own words,"* and "liberty and justice for *all.*"

Good evening, my fellow citizens:

This Government, as promised,
has maintained the closest surveillance
of the Soviet military build-up on the
island of Cuba. Within the past week,
unmistakable evidence has established
the fact that a series of offensive
missile sites is now in preparation
on that imprisoned island. The
purpose of these bases can be none
other than to provide a nuclear strike
capability against the Western
Hemisphere.   Upon receiving the first
preliminary hard information of this
nature last Tuesday morning at 9 a.m.,

I directed that our surveillance be stepped up. And having now confirmed and completed our evaluation of the evidence and our decision on a course of action, this Government feels obliged to report this new crisis to you in full detail.

The characteristics of these new missile sites indicate two distinct types of installations. Several of them ~~indicate~~ INCLUDE Medium Range Ballistic Missiles, capable of carrying a nuclear warhead for a distance of more than 1000 nautical miles. Each of these missiles, in short, is capable of striking Washington, D.C.,

the Panama Canal, Cape Canaveral,
Mexico City, or any other city in the
Southeastern part of the United
States, in Central America or in the
Caribbean area.

Additional sites not yet
completed appear to be designed for
Intermediate Range Ballistic
Missiles -- capable of travelling more
than twice as far -- and thus capable
of striking most of the major cities
in the Western Hemisphere, ranging as
far north as Hudson's Bay, Canada
and as far south as Lima, Peru. In
addition, jet bombers, capable of
carrying nuclear weapons,

are now being uncrated and assembled
on Cuba, while the necessary air bases
are being prepared.

This urgent transformation of
Cuba into an important strategic
base -- by the presence of these large,
long-range and clearly offensive
weapons of sudden mass destruction --
constitutes an explicit threat to the
peace and security of all the Americas,
in flagrant and deliberate defiance of
the Rio Pact of 1947, the traditions of
this nation and Hemisphere, the Joint
Resolution of the 87th Congress, the
Charter of the United Nations, and my
own public warnings to the Soviets on
September 4 and 13.

This action also contradicts the
repeated assurances of Soviet
spokesmen, both publicly and privately
delivered, that the arms build-up in
Cuba would retain its original defensiv
character, and that the Soviet Union ha:
no need or desire to station strategic
missiles on the territory of any other
nation.

The size of this undertaking makes
clear that it had been planned some
months ago. Yet only last month, after
I had made clear the distinction betweer
any introduction of ground-to-ground
missiles and the existence of defensive
anti-aircraft missiles,

the Soviet Government publicly stated
on September 11 that "the armaments
and military equipment sent to Cuba
are designed exclusively for defensive
purposes", that "there is no need for
the Soviet Union to shift its
weapons . . . for a retaliatory blow
to any other country, for instance
Cuba", and that "the Soviet Union has
so powerful rockets to carry these
nuclear warheads that there is no need
to search for sites for them beyond the
boundaries of the Soviet Union." That
statement was false.

Only last Thursday, as evidence of
this rapid offensive build-up was
already in my hand,

Soviet Foreign Minister Gromyko told
me in my office that he was instructed
to make it clear once again, as he
said his Government had already done,
that Soviet assistance to Cuba
"pursued solely the purpose of
contributing to the defense
capabilities of Cuba", that "training
by Soviet specialists of Cuban
nationals in handling defensive
armaments was by no means offensive",
and that "if it were otherwise, the
Soviet Government would never become
involved in rendering such assistance."
That statement also was false.

8

Neither the United States of
America nor the world community of
nations can tolerate deliberate
deception and offensive threats on
the part of any nation, large or small.
We no longer live in a world where
only the actual firing of weapons
represents a sufficient challenge to
a nation's security to constitute a
maximum peril. Nuclear weapons are so
destructive, and ballistic missiles are
so swift, that any substantially
increased possibility of their use or
any sudden change in their deployment
may well be regarded as a definite
threat to the peace.

For many years, both the Soviet Union and the United States -- recognizing this fact -- have deployed strategic nuclear weapons with great care, never upsetting the precarious status quo which ensured that these weapons would not be used in the absence of some vital challenge. Our own strategic missiles have never been transferred to the territory of any other nation under a cloak of secrecy and deception; and our history -- unlike that of the Soviets since World War II -- demonstrates that we have no desire to dominate or conquer any other nation or impose our system upon its people.

Nevertheless, American citizens have
become adjusted to living daily on
the bull's eye of Soviet missiles
located inside the USSR or in
submarines. In that sense, missiles
in Cuba add to an already clear and
present danger -- although, it should
be noted, the nations of Latin America
have never previously been subjected
to a potential nuclear threat.

But this secret, swift and
extraordinary build-up of communist
missiles -- in an area well-known to
have a special and historical
relationship to the United States and
the nations of the Western Hemisphere,

in violation of Soviet assurances,
and in defiance of American and
Hemispheric policy -- this sudden,
clandestine decision to station
strategic weapons for the first time
outside of Soviet soil -- is a
deliberately provocative and
unjustified change in the status quo
which cannot be accepted by this
country, if our courage and our
commitments are ever to be trusted
again by either friend or foe.

The 1930's taught us a clear
lesson: aggressive conduct, if allowed
to grow unchecked and unchallenged,
ultimately leads to war. This nation
is opposed to war.

12

We are also true to our word. Our
unswerving objective, therefore,
must be to prevent the use of these
missiles against this or any other
country, and to secure their
withdrawal or elimination from the
Western Hemisphere.

Our policy has been one of
patience and restraint, as befits a
peaceful and powerful nation, which
leads a world-wide alliance. We have
been determined not to be diverted
from our central concerns by mere
irritants and fanatics. But now
further action is required -- and
it is underway; and these actions
may only be the beginning.

We will not prematurely or
unnecessarily risk the costs of
world-wide nuclear war in which
even the fruits of victory would
be ashes in our mouth -- but neither
will we shrink from that risk at
any time it must be faced.

Acting, therefore, in the
defense of our own security and that
of the entire Western Hemisphere,
and under the authority entrusted
to me by the Constitution as
endorsed by the Resolution of the
Congress, I have directed that the
following <u>initial</u> steps be taken
immediately:

1) _First_: to halt this
offensive build-up, a strict
quarantine on all offensive
military equipment under shipment
to Cuba is being initiated. All
ships of any kind bound for Cuba,
from whatever nation or port, will,
if found to contain cargoes of
offensive weapons, be turned back.
This quarantine will be extended,
if needed, to other types of cargo
and carriers. We are not at this
time, however, denying the necessities
of life as the Soviets attempted to do
in their Berlin blockade of 1948.

2) <u>Second</u>: I have directed the continued and increased close surveillance of Cuba and its military build-up. The Foreign Ministers of the OAS in their communique of October 6 rejected secrecy on such matters in this Hemisphere. Should these offensive military PREPARATIONS ~~preparations~~ continue, thus increasing the threat to the Hemisphere, further action will be justified. I have directed the armed forces to prepare for any eventualities; and I trust that, in the interest of both the Cuban people and the Soviet technicians at these sites, the hazards to all concerned of continuing this threat will be recognized.

3) <u>Third</u>: It shall be the policy of this nation to regard any nuclear missile launched from Cuba against any nation in the Western Hemisphere as an attack by the Soviet Union on the United States requiring a full retaliatory response upon the Soviet Union.

4) <u>Fourth</u>: As a necessary military precaution, I have reinforced our base at Guantanamo, evacuated today the dependents of our personnel there and ordered additional military units to stand by on an alert basis.

5) <u>Fifth</u>: We are calling tonight for an immediate meeting of the Organ of Consultation under the Organization of American States,

to consider this threat to
hemispheric security and to invoke
Articles 6 and 8 of the Rio Treaty in
support of all necessary action. The
United Nations Charter allows for
regional security arrangements -- and
the nations of this hemisphere decided
long ago against the military presence
of outside powers. Our other allies
around the world have also been
alerted.

6) <u>Sixth</u>: Under the Charter of th
United Nations, we are asking tonight
that an emergency meeting of the
Security Council be convoked without
delay to take action against this
latest Soviet threat to world peace.

Our Resolution will call for the prompt
dismantling and withdrawal of all
offensive weapons in Cuba, under the
supervision of UN observers, before the
quarantine can be lifted.

7) <u>Seventh and finally</u>: I call
upon Chairman Khrushchev to halt and
eliminate this clandestine, reckless
and provocative threat to world peace
and to stable relations between our
two nations. I call upon him further
to abandon this course of world
domination, and to join in an historic
effort to end the perilous arms race
and transform the history of man. He
has an opportunity now to move the world
back from the abyss of destruction --

by returning to his government's own
words that it had no need to station
missiles outside its own territory,
and withdrawing these weapons from
Cuba -- by refraining from any action
which will widen or deepen the present
crisis -- and then by participating
in a search for peaceful and permanent
solutions.

This nation is prepared to
present its case against this Soviet
threat to peace, and our own proposals
for a peaceful world, at any time and
in any forum -- in the OAS, in the
United Nations, or in any other
meeting that could be useful --
without limiting our freedom of action.

We have in the past made strenuous
efforts to limit the spread of nuclear
weapons. We have proposed the
elimination of all arms and military
bases in a fair and effective
disarmament treaty. We are prepared
to discuss new proposals for the
removal of tensions on both sides --
including the possibilities of a
genuinely independent Cuba, free to
determine its own destiny. We have
no wish to war with the Soviet Union --
for we are a peaceful people who
desire to live in peace with all other
peoples.

But it is difficult to settle
or even discuss these problems in an
atmosphere of intimidation.

That is why this latest Soviet threat --
or any other threat which is made
either independently or in response
to our actions this week -- must and
will be met with determination. Any
hostile move anywhere in the world
against the safety and freedom of
peoples to whom we are committed --
including in particular the brave
people of West Berlin -- will be met
by whatever action is needed.

Finally, I want to say a few
words to the captive people of Cuba,
to whom this speech is being directly
carried by special radio facilities.
I speak to you as a friend, as one who
knows of your deep attachment to your
fatherland,

as one who shares your aspirations
for liberty and justice for all.
And I have watched with deep sorrow
how your nationalist revolution was
betrayed -- and how your fatherland
fell under foreign domination. Now
your leaders are no longer Cuban
leaders inspired by Cuban ideals.
They are puppets and agents of an
international conspiracy which has
turned Cuba against your friends and
neighbors in the Americas -- and turned
it into the first Latin American
country to become a target for nuclear
war -- the first Latin American country
to have these weapons on its soil.

These new weapons are not in your interest. They contribute nothing to your peace and well-being. They can only undermine it. But this country has no wish to cause you to suffer or to impose any system upon you. We know your lives and land are being used as pawns by those who deny you freedom.

Many times in the past, the Cuban people have risen to throw out tyrants who destroyed their liberty. And I have no doubt that most Cubans today look forward to the time when they will be truly free -- free from foreign domination, free to choose their own leaders,

free to select their own system,
free to own their own land, free to
speak and write and worship without
fear or degradation. And then shall
Cuba be welcomed back to the society
of free nations and to the associations
of this Hemisphere.

* * *

My fellow citizens: let no one
doubt that this is a difficult and
dangerous effort on which we have set
out. No one can foresee precisely
what course it will take or what costs
or casualties will be incurred. Many
months of sacrifice and self-discipline
lie ahead -- months in which both our
will and our patience will be tested --

months in which many threats and
denunciations will keep us aware of
our danger. But the greatest danger
of all would be to do nothing.

The path we have chosen for the
present is full of hazards, as all
paths are -- but it is the one most
consistent with our character and
courage as a nation and our
commitments around the world. The
cost of freedom is always high --
but Americans have always paid it.
And one path we shall never choose
is the path of surrender or submission.

Our goal is not the victory of
might but the vindication of right --
not peace at the expense of freedom,

26

but both peace <u>and</u> freedom, here in

this Hemisphere, and, we hope,

around the world.   God willing,

that goal will be achieved.

* * *

FOR FURTHER READING:

Kennedy, Robert F. *Thirteen Days*. New York: W. W. Norton & Co., 1969. The final two chapters are particularly illuminating.

[Khrushchev, Nikita]. Trans. and ed. by Strobe Talbott. *Khrushchev Remembers*. Boston: Little, Brown and Co., 1970.

Schlesinger, Arthur M. *A Thousand Days*. Boston: Houghton Mifflin Co., 1965.

Sorensen, Theodore. *Kennedy*. New York: Harper & Row, 1965.